VIEW from the GAZEBO

WESLEYAN NEW POETS

VIEW from the GAZEBO

Marianne Boruch (signature)

MARIANNE BORUCH

WESLEYAN UNIVERSITY PRESS

Middletown, Connecticut

I wish to thank the National Endowment for the Arts for the fellowship and the Wisconsin Arts Board for the project grant that made the completion of this book possible.

Some of the poems in this book appeared originally in the following journals, some in an earlier form: *Abraxas*, "Writing in the Presence of a Wounded Bird"; *American Poetry Review*, "Gazing at the Pigs," "Her Early Darkness," "Late Summer," "Letter," "The Violinist Beginning to Fly"; *The Antioch Review*, "Static"; *Beloit Poetry Journal*, "Sympathy"; *Field*, "First Snow," "The Furniture of Light," "Her Brown Checked Dress," "I Put On My Jonathan Edwards This Apple Season," "Stranger in Your Room," "We Drove"; *Indiana Review*, "Grief"; *Iowa Review*, "Diamond Breakfast," "On Translation," "Passage"; *The Little Magazine*, "A Line Is Just a Series of Dots"; *Mississippi Review*, "To the Leaf-Mad Treehouse," "View from the Gazebo, 1914"; *New Letters*, "Secrets"; *Partisan Review*, "The Blue-Black Light"; *Ploughshares*, "The Blue Chair," "The Fortune Teller," "The Hammer Falls, Is Falling," "Memory Biscuit"; *Prairie Schooner*, "This Moment of Raven"; *Some*, "Chicago Poultry."

This book is supported by a grant from the National Endowment for the Arts.

LIBRARY OF CONGRESS CATALOGING IN PUBLICATION DATA

Boruch, Marianne, 1950–
   View from the gazebo.

   I. Title.
PS3552.O75645V5   1985   811'.54   84-20834
ISBN 0-8195-2125-6
ISBN 0-8195-1126-9 (pbk.)

All inquiries and permission requests should be addressed to the Publisher, Wesleyan University Press, 110 Mt. Vernon Street, Middletown, Connecticut 06457.

Distributed by Harper & Row Publishers, Keystone Industrial Park, Scranton, Pennsylvania 18512.

Manufactured in the United States of America

First Edition

Wesleyan New Poets

FOR DAVID

Contents

I

II

III

I

View from the Gazebo, 1914

Late June & the bees came
violent, rising off the far hedge
in busy black hooks.
We too were busy
lemonade busy, day to day
and porchlight busy
so busy we thought them
hummingbirds
that nervous race
which overruns the afternoon
with wonder, graceful creatures
soundlessly
emptying the rose.
Such stillness.
My father closed his book
with a low whistle.
These bees
finding our clover thin
our thickets barely ripe
angered. In the silent brain
of the gazebo, my parents froze
elegant & empty-handed
Victorians at the edge of sleep.
This heady mob rushing toward us
an ancient mesh, dark and light
crushed against the wind, I thought
the world is ending.

Her Early Darkness

She remembers kneading, the grim
thrust: fists, then open hands. Dough
she twists, earmarks, flattens,
pounds. The sound of violent
meditation. She calls what possesses her
blue light in the veins; she calls it
her toughened grain.

Yeast, the small animal world
in a brown glass jar. Oxygen-eaters.
Every day the lid tightens. Yeast
into flour, she says, like breath
returning to the pale body
of a swimmer, gone out too far
too long. A crowd waits in a circle
heads down. His first heave
they pull from him
with little sucking noises. Yeast
making sounds with its mouth
of large bubbles.

Bread baking. Bread breaking out
of wheat, water, salt. Her quiet lungs
compressed, ready to spring. Breath
of wheat filling the kitchen, blue light
drained from the window and leaving her.

Krakow and the Girl of Twelve

The dog downstairs is howling back
to the old country. My grandmother
bends to pick up the hoe
drags it, sun-slant, down toward the field
kicking the blunt end
up, until it flashes.

> *Wolves*, her mother said,
slipping through the gate.

The Blue-Black Light

A child with a gun
is parting the bushes next to the house
his foot dropping steadily
over stones, over darkened grass.
Breathing is difficult as the moment
nears
      I put down my book
in this blue-black light, as if water
could or needed to be
read. What was I thinking: *remote*
possible. I know that
stirring, how quick it happens
now the child
slipping out of the leaves
not a shadow at all
but a thought
        slipping out of its mind
sucking up the room
as I sit swearing I
haven't heard a human voice for years.
The trees wild, small winds
ruthless in their courage
          the child
trembles on the walkway
           what shiny
thing in the heart surrenders
or is opaque.

The Moon Losing Its Color
All Over the Street

A woman is taking off her clothes and putting on
her feathers. Darkness fools
a town like this. Her watch, her shoes
lie glowing on the grass.
                              I am living
in an attic heart
across the street. My breath
comes blue. Her feathers, one by one, as birds
sink into human dream like fossil
stones, with wings pinned up
to fly. She's old. The body folds that quietly
into air.
             I've cleared
the window soot. Her silver deepens red.
I think I'm falling
through her. I am seeping into
trees behind her.
                        How gold she looks, how frail!
this opera night. She is whizzing
into hum of human wing
against the time to sleep and eat
and live a human life.
                              She is larger
than the mind, between the clouds
a cloudy thought
taking off her clothes and putting on her feathers.
                              It takes a tree
to imagine such a thing
as leaves, but a woman, a woman
falling through me. I've stopped
breathing in the dark,
                        the moon . . .

7

Diamond Breakfast

Overnight, the windows have multiplied & eaten
the house. Boom! everything
is thinner, everything
manic with light. "Whirling dervish!" whispers
mother, screwing up her eyes
into little eyes. The children
lean like cactus in the doorway. Maybe
they are missing school. O rodeo, O Oklahoma shimmer.

Father clears his throat. "Things
are different now," he says, addressing the squints
from the breakfast nook. "That stove, for instance,
these eggs—all just a glimmer
of their former selves. Remember this.
This is like history." One boy agrees. He is
shielding his eyes as if an iceberg
has surfaced, he is planting
a blue flag.

Now they are eating, drinking: glossy oatmeal,
shiny milk. Everything is a ghastly color. White & white
& white again. Outside, birds dive
into invisible walls
their small heads dashed against pure thought.

The Violinist Beginning to Fly

—after Chagall

They plan to get him down
a loop of thread
pulled from his trousers and the only way
says the doctor
of willfulness and logic, a coppery icon
rooted and lit
above the leather bag growing
smaller as we walk away.

From this distance, the violinist is drifting
straight into the sun: just a man
fiddling his brains out, say—joy bundle of nerves,
say—man disbelieving the dark secret, say—roof light
in a bottle and he's drinking it.
Think about his heartbeat then, slow as anyone's
who, searching and searching, finds
the perfect place to live. These bits of Handel
bracing the air, or letting it go, not
going to the dogs but just stepping outside: here

a dazed summer night, the screen door
banging behind, lily of the valley in the walkway,
inevitable smell of rain. Ah—so many things finally

not to care about.

Love Poem Against the Spring

Spring means nothing but camouflage
so we dare to say these corny things. Irrelevant birds
smokescreen up the afternoon & purple flowers
rear up their idiot faces along the sidewalk's edge.
OK, they're cute. My hunger's not, nor my ache
at you green-leafed and alert somewhere, not here.
Perhaps the pretty air
exaggerates some things. I see, a friend annunciates,
you *access* him—as if you were a computer.
Last night I saw three couples, incredible throwbacks,
strolling into dusk, two so giddy, they'd love anything.
I'm quiet as a brick. But for spring
this far I'd go—glad, I guess, to shed this coat. It's you
I crave, you who get more stunning
as we age.

A Line Is Just a Series of Dots

I was swelling up with Euclid
my sophomore year. Our thick tweed jackets

hung like captured ghosts. It seemed
a winter book: face value, spare,

fueled by white bones. Next to me, Curry
popped jellybeans in her Twiggy cut, daydreaming

roses or rowdy John York. But I was
heartsure, floating in the third seat, these

were magic tools: protractor & compass. Did they
shine in the dark? I never looked. I knew.

Sister Francis gummed her words. "It doesn't happen
happenstance." And we, alert as blue grass,

stared into the eerie page, where triangles & squares
held their breath in open air. This is

our secret life, I thought, as line moved
onto line, as gardens focused

in the awful mist. I was swelling up
with Euclid, pure thread all that endless spring

trailing proofs to their treasure, an inevitable
cloud, an inevitable clearing.

Standing by Your Grave Without
a Lot of Questions

—for my grandfather

A sled, you murmured toward the end.
We thought that a joke too. After all, light bulb
blew and kitchen surged, darkness
sucking in such a full creature, you said we
could build a boat of it and float for years
on what was left. Now, old man, I'd give

millions to thump thump thump you up
but it's your buzz that stays me, your
skeletal rasp, as you grasped the flowered chair,
"more god-damn junk," pointing down
our Ouija board, "don't try me after I'm fled
this place, I'll nightmare you!" Some days

I fix the eggs the wretched way you
liked: the bacon soggy, whites
trembling, the uncertain yolk. Is that
a meditation? Then this long walk here's
meditation too. Plantain and dandelion

bend light above your head. I really don't
know how to miss you. I walk three times
around your grave. And three more times.
Birds sit hunched and nervous
across the yard. You'd laugh at them,
boo them baffled into air.

The Cheerful Light of July

The solemn luxury of a fall day
is memory already, birds sepia
in their certain journey out of sight. We look up
cold morning, afternoon, the gray sweater weight
thinning the trespass of wind and stupidity.
I'm imagining this
in summer as leaves gaze blankly into sun,
as kids downtown
skateboard the minutes
until supper and it's still light outside
as we eat. I hate summer, which is beauty
so transparent, a wealth so true and trusting
I cannot believe but backdrop
bright easel to narrow in the wharf, the fleeting boats.
I think: snow, snow and the mind
invents storms that come, leaves
turning violent, red and yellow
out of sheer boredom
with the slow pitch of a summer month.
I put on my shoes and go outside.
Cheerful light of July where no death creeps
which makes me nervous—these boats
taking their time on the perfect lake, ferry
their pleasure out, then home again
and so disguise, disguise, disguise.

Writing in the Presence of
a Wounded Bird

The disaster speaks of its hero
with a desperate harp, a hollow log
leading the logjam, finally
downriver to its farthest depth.
It's a clean night, those first minutes
when the forest becomes just
a bunch of trees
standing below a dark sky, stars
waking as they always do, with a certain
grace, with a certain hopelessness. I took
that river once, saw the water
as anything but, thinking: words
are like this if you stare long enough.
I wondered about room in my heart
for the thing itself, sincere water
where the postcards give out.

That quiet is what I memorize
when the engine
dies and snow covers
the windshield. The music of it
walks me from the parking lot
to the house, where the phone
slips into a real phone and the clear
thought of me calling
opens the empty air.

We Drove

to the end of the world in a real
nice car, red upholstery
and the gasoline scent of childhood filling
the whole back seat with darkness
and lemonade and the drive-in already
starting, screen flicker
of power and bosom, Dad lifting the bright box
hero-voice
spurting into the old Chevy.
We had these pale pajamas, curling
sideways, we followed the beam
through its gaudy lifetime
blue greens focused
then blurred
a lady's red lips flung
open against the final second. We knew
nothing of this, or the moon's
double color, jouncing every which way

home, silent, half-
happy the thing over and sleep
a real one
taking off his hat, past railroad
dumps, houses here and there
glowing in the fields
Dad's filibuster of neighbors
and melancholy friends, the wide
roar, everything
winding down
to a pin, the original
night.

Letter

When the final cricket stops
—a few moments ago
this part word, that part
nothing refinable—
what is written
lengthens: the light
of the moon's rare
thought. Yesterday I thought
you'd be whistling toward me
delighted as usual
with a simple supper—rice,
bits of beef, something
thin & leafy.
I sensed you coming
a moment ago. I almost
heard your whistle
some fine Puccini knife
cutting the whole
dark, field
cramping up behind you
a heavy bulk
chewing up your passage
which was light
as usual, musical.
The crevice deepens
around the house. Yesterday
half-earth, half-air, workmen
stood and blankly shoveled
in the sun. I bolted out
of sleep with this, as if
the drift had started
as if the neighbor's house

the field you love
had dwindled, and
in the distance, darkened.
Step wide
when you return
too late to see
this thing which
strangers dug
which scares me.

Late Summer

After lunch, we spread ourselves like laundry
to be bleached or dried, dozing
funny, sort of upright
against that hill. Behind your house, those
fields. We watched them break
into longer grass.
We could launch a boat, but I
imagined this. It was simply wind.

I stared into the earth as trees darkened
a long white road in Greece: you were talking
us everywhere but here, these
specks of life below my hand
winged weird dust, some
with eyes. They will die. I turned

you had taken off your sweater, an undershirt
dipped, your breast
so small
lit with that terrible quiet
something lovely has. I gazed
into my hands as if a boat
would dock there. Late summer
spun around us like a dye.

Grief

A woman is hauling silence
into the house.
Such a serious rope
a dangerous glass eye.
I see a forest
in her mind, this close to me,
a lightning storm
moving over the brook.

I have to shut the window, the woman says.
I have to sleep.

She takes a leaf and strikes
a wooden match. She is
so far from here, holding the leaf
above her head,
in the other waiting hand, the flame.

She stands forever
in the middle of the thing.

Her Brown Checked Dress

I open the door to this room
flooded with childhood, *just going about our business*
my grandmother before the dresser mirror
curling iron in hand.
I am the girl, twirling on the tall footboard
just a kid, a punk
watching as a child watches, how long till supper
till sleep, till school. She is small,
she steps into a brown checked dress, smoothing it down
bony thing, hopeless
to look right, she says, giving it up, taking powder
to her face. My uncle's young
and in a frame
smiling as he never smiles. I am telling about
Vickie and what she said to Glenna
about that boy. We discuss it carefully, the way
chess is played
on a deeply shadowed porch. Midsummer, 1959
and I become a ghost to find her.
Here is my body.
Here are my useless shoes.

II

Stranger in Your Room

Late that day, old woman
nothing pulsed. The bike got stiff.
Long miles, I ached it
home, up the freezing driveway

paused, past your window where
you read as usual
the hazel glow of lamp
all winter, words
you stubbornly

clung to. But the curly-headed stranger
poised in darkness
on the pale divan, only
I could see him
across from you, his head cupped
those hands, ice blue: *should I*
Is she that

I stepped back. How
carelessly you turned the page!
as if roof
could hold the dark dead weight
wind up, snow
shifting so
against the house.

The Death Odes

he is taking your mattress
out into the yard
where rain will enter your sleep
and sleep is leaking
like an old oil drum
he is dragging your mattress
down the narrow stair
cursing the corners
you are doing nothing
but waiting below
arms folded
looking up

I

Death is different from the bird
the child says
paraphrasing the teacher
it has no nest for instance
how does it live
the child adjusts his glasses
Death is part of the lake
brimming with weeds
how does it live
midsummer, someone tries
out there with a scythe
harvesting the bloated grass
how does it
even early morning
cup the lake in your hands
its dark grains
some sinking fast, some floating

2

Gravity. Death is amused
that long leash
even men outwitting the moon
think they must have it
pulling it up from the earth
I am not the monster
sinking this steam locomotive
into the butter air

3

Already it is autumn
before the glossy catalog
Death is only silent
everything will last forever
resolable shoes reinforced seams
Death following the delivery man
the young lawyer
razors the box
the boots gleam in the darkened hall
o leaf you are wiser
entering the seed at once
where Death is a stranger
no, cannot come

4

In a crowd
it is hard to pick out Death
he is so pleasant and the eye moves first
to the raving the ruthless
who wear their jaws

at an angle closing slowly
on the acid in their mouths
there
against this flawless human head
filling the earth with every solitude
where you cannot fit even a finger
too small for him
Death is wearing such a hat

5

Meanwhile here is a rug
Death is weaving
the child says a TV
all the favorites: Big Bird & Kermit
all day the rug is woven electric
on the eye the lives of strangers
who never stop talking
how much for this rug covering
the cold floor
thickening the house
how much
adamant Death
smiling his excuse

6

Do not believe these accidents
Death does not drink
the way we do
does not enter a car
after sad conversations
think: how darkness reroutes the world
and the moon

a distant nonsense
Death renting a room over the street
under the name Anderson or Bailey
Death forgetful
leaning over the ledge watching
those he has no right
young girls yet
crossing into the movies
our drab car
for one sudden moment
blocking his view

Distant Knowledge
Which Spits and Flashes

Whatever distance a man considers
he picks up the telescope
to change it. I would bring you closer
if I could, as flipping on the radio
brings the 18th century into the room: Bach
wallpaper and oranges, old bedspread
and scissors of Bach, suddenly
corduroy of Bach turning into a shirt
as I fiddle with the bobbin
against the cold teeth of this machine.
I think of the machine
that took you, dazzling car
midwinter, and I think you back centuries
before words were invented
to explain your death, or the car, or the broken asphalt.
Angel of logic, distant knowledge
which spits and flashes. Change it if I could
picking up this telescope
to zoom you back, here
for a simple talk
but there are stars where you are.
Their passion blinds you.

First Snow

My grandfather is dying again
all day as rain widens
slipping into snow like the adolescent kid
gone haywire overnight
taller then, not terribly handsome
just knocking over chairs.
I pick up that chair for the thirteenth time
trying to find the old man
gone silent on the porch, staring
as if the window could stare back, as if kids
still sledded their brains out, evergreens
holding aloft their sad fierce secrets about everything.
So I hear him in my head: did I tell you?
Buffalo Bill on the train. That one.
No, I'd say. Tell me.
It's been November now for too many days, the month that empties
itself cold into harbors, the month
stalled there among weeds and the sleep-locked boats.
But sitting in this chair again
I could take every bland bit of it
into my arms, brother forgiveness,
sister indifference. This pause between fall
and the inevitable dead weight
bearing down the beauty of a January day.
Say simply: here I am
and there a stranger waits across from me, closing up
a life so quietly the fall of dust could deafen us.
Or so I sit, arms out as if I could catch him
his eyes turning back
until a kid sleds right into them
1883 or so, breathlessness intact.
No, I say, tell me. Tell me.

The Blue Chair

The leaves have their own civilization.
I won't say decline. What they do is starve
and the brilliant yellows, red, porcelain coppers of these days
beg for nothing more, but
die quietly. I walk the streets
on their behalf, holding my heart up
like a bowl, and falling, they fall

as a boat falls into its groaning oar. Now the bird
delaying on a branch. I have heard
that call in the bright stubble: cowboy relic,
hermit pain of beauty, as one voice
travels cave to cave and flutters

finally in my hands. I pick up this blue chair,
take it to the window. Nothing. Details.
A tree. A fence. A sudden dog.
On the garage roof, the wind is finally free.
I picture it again—*free*—as if we all believe

in such a boat, our crying out
in sleep, our own dark motioning to shore.

Passage

I took the old man in me
& went to the river.
Get out, I said
opening my coat
to tree & air & ice.
Get out, I said. This is it.

He would not look at me.
Blunt feather
as he moved, dark trace
spine & rib.
I thought: you sullen bird,
you fish. I imagined his blue eyes, hook
simple, hard as dice. I swore
above the glare: teach me now, bastard.
                               Thin pajamas, stepping
into wind.

I buttoned my coat
as he walked toward the water.
For a moment, his hair
flashed
impossibly white. I thought of river filth
his numb, pale weight
                          dropping into the cold jaw.
I opened my mouth: *nothing   nothing.*

Falling Asleep to Voices

A room drifts into evening like a boat
is slow, carrying up a long sadness
from childhood
those two silver oars.
I can barely make them out
straining to remember
as furniture disappears
as voices of neighbors
up from the yard below
go laughter, go so many stones upon a bell
fish within fish
until all of it is water.
I'm sure now, sure
I've been floating like this
every summer for 33 years.
I lie down in it. I close my eyes
rising on the disembodied sound—leaves too,
hesitant in the wind
a hammer falling, a child bouncing a ball.
Lovely world
which has no body, just voice, just
darkness, what we crave in it
distance—a curse
as blurred as a kiss
as splendid, as irrelevant.
I pull the covers up
hoping this is death.

Violin

A boy begins to play
a rose too red
for the empty hall.
Tremor of resin and bow
I lie down in it to love this boy
until the distance is old, old
the violin puts between us.
Always the overheard, the eavesdrop, the accidental gift
so the violin is forever
talking to itself, and those who hear
grow embarrassed, moved beyond reason
to the edge of things: that secret of stillness
in the bird who flies. I am older for it,
by the minute, older. Old Auntie with her blue gloves on.
I cross my feet just so, I fold my arms
until I see
the outstretched hand, the handkerchief, the tattered sleeve.
But I say: no, Death.
This boy has come between us.
You can take your peace. There are other roses
pale, silent
where it belongs.

This Moment of Raven

I stand in the middle of the road
but I don't know it's a road
only in hindsight is this possible

saying then, I stood in the middle of a road
leaf-light but thickening
with summer as a man up ahead

walks beside his horse   *it's all right, steady*
taking the hand
of the child beside him. In hindsight then, I

imagine this 100 years ago, this
in hindsight, that it's sensible
for a man to calm a horse

that would carry him, the child who
will bury him but tenderness
clouds the moment

out of hindsight into this raven
who takes me into his heart
whispering: watch this man this horse this child

you know them.

How Quiet the Town

The womb, flashing its own
blue light.
I sit down quietly before it.
So cool in here. Churchish.
Bones in the sun vanish.
A long damp grass
nudges toward the water.

So this is my monster, I think.
A blue trance
which begins all beginnings
melting
everything stranger
than the first embryo wish to be
strange & breathing
is bluer. My hands lie translucent
dozing near their river-veins.

We came this way: a pin of light
wheeling
its iridescence into the newborn street.
How quiet the town. No one awake.

To the Leaf–Mad Treehouse

I put myself strange, pretend
we are old friends this tree
and I age rapidly
wood beams, leaf lights the broken wall
it's been years, I say, years

trying to be swell, water
dozing in the root-warm cellar. Distant
rain, distant friendless detail: nothing really
boats us in, old tree
nothing curls. I take my hand

to hand, lay flat
these floorboards, chant
ghost yeast finally
                    this is how how
leaf-mad wisdom
buckled, burst the dark. I pretend the wood
is simple, single hammer, finite nails.
Someone lived here simply. Rag
and bone it all.

Secrets

After three weeks of rain
the car is a perfect piece of rust
a monster, a miracle
of chemical reactions. The old man
whose car it is
calls his wife to the window
just as moonlight
leans its chin on the front fender.
Look at that, says the woman, a sleeping chin.
Look at that, a dove walk. Her hands
flicker in a secret wind, her lips
barely move.

Who let the air in? Everything—the rake, the roof
the evening sky aches with a strange joy
as if let out of jail for the first time.
The car soaks up the whole yard.

Dog Music

While we sleep, the dog is dying
rising from the curl of fur & years, a flicker
in the slow dark rising without our waking or knowing.
We breathe but the air is hers. Eddy or glow wave,
she is the drift of an old dollar
blowing out to sea. A moment ago—am I dreaming this—
her shadow fell full mast: flag or strange egg
breaking over us, now passing through the door
where the kitchen waits
like a new world. Refrigerator life! She sails
the electric gloom, hum
of an old hum. The heartbeat disappears.

Memory Biscuit

Everyone's real world is a memory biscuit
lodged somewhere in the spine
or the ribs—a question of how one
sits, when a strange kid is howling
and you're thinking: now *my* kid will be interested
in the classics.

Meanwhile, the biscuit dreams,
pulp of childhood and lumpy adolescence
nudging its way to the table
after years
of hanging around: just the kitchen, just
the corny backyard.
Voilà! a four-course dinner
under American trees. What a bang
to start with—lime jello on lettuce. Sometimes
everything on earth
seems edible. Sometimes everyone in you
is eating.

Bird Census

The town was obsessed with birds
how many and who and wherever
they went during winter. An ad in the *Courier*
begging for bird-wise, sensible shoes, we will pay,
please appear with a solid lunch all
sighters who dapple the woods with their sneaky love
a sudden breath
at the flash of a heron bathing
where the forest drops from ordinary wonder, but
I paraphrase, grow waxy. They were, in fact,

a ruthless bunch: Mr. Sausage
& rugged Long John and the larger mad librarians
of every age. But my Peterson! My opera glasses!
I was awestruck, stuck at the end of the line, through pines
then maples, they discussed ferns, or dark remains
of ferns: *Matteuccia Struthiopteris, Onoclea Sensibilis*, I thought
Virgil's calling his sheep home, as we Romans
forge. Britain! Horrible Snow!
endless and oh, what a night
our rations low, Captain, O Captain, our
fearful trip is done, done! Duck!

shot Aragon Pound, and the Quaker Lady, second in command,
lowered her hand. We held our silence
like a box of mints. It didn't look
like a duck. I crouched in the unpronounceable
bones of foliage. Killer red, my brother would call it
holding his hand to his eyes, peeking was piercing
color in that shaded rush of snow. A small bird
idled. What *was* he doing? Thinking, probably, having
a nice dream: worm sandwiches, sugared water
for all. I wasn't that

crazy about him; he looked obnoxious—really—as if
the redder reds had huffed: all right for you,
Pill. Still, he didn't startle.
Stage Presence. I admired that, a form of belief
not at all embarrassing in a bird. But it was me
who wondered, caught between air and water
not knowing how to swim or fly. I eyed
the other watchers eyeing him, their fabulous strain,
inaudible pencils: female, young, indicates
hundreds of others. "Hundreds" in this

drowsy wasteland? A wacky over-
abundance of human hope. I hoped they'd gone
south, Gidget feasting on egg rolls & Moondoggie
whisking off the blanket for the 89th time. Ah, such crumbs!
Beer, baloney and rye. In the distance, more
distance, the sea rattling its light and secret and a whole slew
of killer reds hoarding the rocks
in a single-minded sate. My god, who were these people.
I felt instant gloom. A bird exception. Bird blues. I didn't have

a pencil. Shhh! one said. The bird began to move
fanned out, a blur
of red pitched into the branches. She began
to sing. But they never sing, Aragon
hissed, the Quaker thumbed
her book, Long John trembled: maybe it's
a different sort of bird.
                    Maybe it's not a bird at all, I said
too gaily. They reported only
my shoes: *not sensible.*

On Translation

The hungry man in the blue hat
has borrowed his ghost   no
the ghost in the borrowed hat just
sat down to dinner. The dinner's really something
is, all extraordinary, it is, more than that, well
a secret, shhh! A lobster who did not die of fright.
"So this one went willingly!" says the ghost
with the borrowed tongue. "Oh yes oh yes oh yes,"
chants a chorus of waiters pressing a bright fork
into his hand. "Ah, such a big one," thinks the man,
"and such a little fork!" He is eating now
reading, between bites, a small round book.
Perhaps the ghost of a book. It is hard to describe
but suddenly, as I watch, I see
the ghost of a lobster beneath the blue hat
rising, rising on a wave
which curls into itself. Something happens
in that haunted mouth.

Chicago Poultry

We are fighting because the
man walking around the Loop
with the chicken on his head, that guy
I swear he's got a chicken and, snot, you say
over and over, No   No   as to a child
it's a duck it's a duck it's a duck and I
hoard the table with a terrific shout.
Fuck you. It's a chicken. I know a chicken
when I see a god-damn fucking chicken. I
grew up eating chicken, being chicken,
playing chicken, two legs and two heads
in that god-awful teenage water at Foster
Avenue beach. That's what I hate about you
you tell me right in the face, right in the eye
right under our immediately precious roof.
WHAT   I shout through the silent bottom bible
of the courtoom stack.   Your roots, he
said, are so mediocre.

The Furniture of Light

I sit down in the furniture of light
& seem to fall asleep, except that weird noise
that rustling. Perhaps this isn't
sleep at all but the future
dimly revealing its marvelous pajamas.
I like those stripes really, how
they taper down
to the delicate ankle. I've seen
that ankle before. I raise my pant leg
with trepidation. No—maybe
Auntie Arnita of the butterscotch brownies,
maybe Mrs. Waxworth of St. Eugene's School.
First Grade! My little desk. I could weep
thinking of Bumpo, my guardian angel
sharing my seat. How ugly he was, how kind
offering me the true pencil and that half
of his sandwich, its funny glow. What a brat
I'd become even then, squeamish, shaking my head,
heart exploding nothing, ribs falling apart. Idiot!
Think if I had eaten the thing. Now
what flowers would pass into thoughts,
what blooming rapture.   All this saddens
before me, a soggy parade, colors
running from the crepe into the city drains.
I sink down into the furniture, getting
sleepy all over again, and the rustle
of pajamas, something
familiar, above the 7–11, on such
a quiet street. Wingbeats! O Bumpo . . .
in a minute, any minute, and me
suddenly so sleepy, these windows darken
with a monstrous light.

I Put On My Jonathan Edwards
This Apple Season

There it is, simplifying the table, everyone
sitting down to apple pie, a pie
reaching back beyond the crust of human anything
a pie of knowledge we invented words for: *knife   fork   pie tin.*
But I put on my Jonathan Edwards & sit
alone, October 23, 1749.
What does it take really, to see
the wolf in that bewildered docile dog
sleeping near the fire. I pick up the napkin again, think
fear fear in that dog's eye
as the wolf creeps unsteadily
from the doggy heart . . . The whole
country, sitting down this minute
a sliver, à la mode, with cheddar. O Ancestor,
lowered right now from the tree, a thought
wrenched from the gloom & glowing darker.

Letter from Taichung

You ask how it is
I can say not good, or
all good, only I am

too lonely, a shut window
the rain beats
blankly against.

Beauty is—
dangerous: whisper of snakes
all summer, their fine poison

flashing through the body
but today, November first
I picture all venom

quietly into sleep. The snake
coiling
under winter's rock

is comfort. You can see
my slow head.
The weather comes cooler

rain in the air
memory
keeping the ruin

alive. Who felled the wall?
I have been reading
an old book

whose cover rots
as I find my way, its spine
shattering

into my lap, the words
Marcus Aurelius, over
then over again

we are breath
bones vanish
forget the imagination.

I ride the bus
into Taichung
the unbearable swell

crowds, motorcycle
& bicycle swarm, all color
a blur of color.

Forget the imagination.
This is merely
a bus, cutting

through the raving
world. Chaos
is enough—the old ghost

tires beside me—float
lightly to death
upon it.

The Fortune Teller

The rest of my life is disguised
in my hand, any intelligence
but mostly confusion
stalking over it, Sumerian tracks
found in some tedious dig
near the holy land.
                        There is a woman now
poised over it. I remember
a dark cloud coming up fast
& dry fields
            corn, soybeans waiting
in a dim happiness. I say

happiness—ridiculous, of course.
Their disguise is what we read, that
faint shiver, leaf-pulse   root   then
rain beginning.

Gazing at the Pigs

They sleep in the flylight
so happily. The violet awning down
midday & a bird

aimlessly alert between the stalls
is the very bird balanced between us
when the child sleeps, or we dream

she is sleeping. I saw once how
your grandfather dozed
beside the radio, that very bird

as he startled awake, a pitch
of blue into the rafters
momentary dark, clouds rushing

the high windows. Look! the pigs
keep grinning, or we dream they do
dreaming of something funny: a pig

chasing a man chasing a wheel
that chases a fat unruly bee
into the thick weeds of the house

where the old man dreams he is
dozing, but he is laughing at the girl
telling the tale—this pig who rushes

the world, weeds blurring, the house
like a hat in the wind, that
very bird beyond them. Gray child

sleep, so thin with flight.

The Hammer Falls, Is Falling

All morning, the man roofs the house
he has dreamt the night before
walking with the wood in his hands
which is growing
as he holds it. The hammer falls, is
falling, one knee bent he
slams the nail
into its silence & out again into the great world
bird, rushing
out of sight, only
a black wing, the look of a wing,
a glimpse of its darkness, nothing.
Stupid, he
bends his knee, stupid. Still the hammer
falls, is falling & the child
he dreamt, putting her to bed, closing the door
under the rude stars, is beginning
to wail, to call up
a word, the man hearing on the roof
the sound of the nail turned bird turned pupil of
darkness watching the air as though
it were breathing.

A Thin Dark Room

this is your heart, I think.
By its brooding, by its simple pain
I know it as a gregarious child
knows loneliness, the life below streets
that sleepwalk
among gasworks and waterlines.
I was that child as you were that child
bodies spent and curled stubbornly
around that vast bleak distance underground
the unhappiness in our heads
brought up hard against it
as a woman matches fabric, square
by various square, against
a recalcitrant brotherhood, the solitude of thread.
Then you turn in sleep.
Shades begin to leak their light.
I watch the smooth beauty of your back
take form, bearings of bone loosen
then nudge tight.
This too is your heart: fall of sun
cold, distinct
the old groundwork
buried gradually and clean.

Static

Two days out & I've lost whatever mind
is kept so clear
by never moving. O runaway car: *almost to Wichita.*
The radio jumps, static
its barbed threat
jarring the fine line, guitar
the voice wire, depression sad
old beater on the last roar home.

I only pretend this is nowhere
as you sit beside me, silent
for several miles. Speed is a kind of knowing,
concrete squeeze, the muscle nerve
& hate it took to lay this road
hypnotic after dark, false, refined
as if the Sunday school
were finally drugged, the brimstone cloud
above us, useless now, but waiting

vagrant as static
eats night air. I take the moon & stare
that we are still awake this late.
Cars, trucks, even wayside places
stubborn in their glow, cling
for a moment, knowledge
as we pray it: night animal wise
brooding bigger
because it's dark. I turn to you

to say it, our lovely
inconsequence anyway. Of course
you sleep.

Sympathy

I drag this big bed to the window
which takes years probably
as the garden spills, as birds darken

the tree outside
slips into her farthest ring, heave
of new bark, water, wood air.

I think she listens so
near the window, pressing
her strange light. I sing

o ragged quilt over the whole world
meaning to say: such is my simple grief
this great dim street

glistening with boys.
How their mothers thin them down
calling them home

quiet baseballs, a few
blue stones. What secrets
in a boy, pitching the last gladness

high into evening: curve
cut, I hear it fallen
at the window, crying to be let in.

About the author

Marianne Boruch grew up in Chicago. She was grad-
uated from the University of Illinois–Urbana (B.S.,
1972) and the University of Massachusetts–Amherst
(M.F.A., 1979) before teaching American literature
at Tunghai University in Taichung, Taiwan, and at the
University of Wisconsin–Madison. She received a fel-
lowship from the National Endowment for the Arts, as
well as Artist-in-Residence and Project grants from the
Wisconsin Arts Board. She teaches in the writing pro-
gram at the University of Maine in Farmington, where
she lives with her husband and young son.

About the book

View from the Gazebo was composed in Bembo by
G & S Typesetters of Austin, Texas. It was printed on 60
lb. Warren's Sebago and bound by Kingsport Press of
Kingsport, Tennessee. Dust jackets and covers were
printed by New England Book Components of Hing-
ham, Massachusetts. Design by Joyce Kachergis Book
Design and Production of Bynum, North Carolina.
Wesleyan University Press, 1985.